The Adventures of Egbert

an entertainment for young violinists
and their friends by
MARY COHEN

PUPIL'S BOOK

FABER MUSIC

3.25

ACKNOWLEDGEMENTS

My thanks to Michael Leckey, Marea Arries and my husband,
Alan Cohen, for all their practical help and encouragement.

The Adventures of Egbert

"Oh *do* hurry up, Egbert!" shouted Mother. "Time for violin practice."
"Practising is boring," grumbled Egbert.
"Well, it needn't be," said Mother. "We could turn it into an ADVENTURE. Let's put a cross on the tip of each finger of your left hand."
"Whatever for?" asked Egbert, still scowling.
"Because all the best treasure maps have 'X marks the spot'. Look . . ."

and she drew this picture.

4 "Long ago," began Mother, "in a far-off country, a wicked King and Queen, Beastly Benedict and Ghastly Gertrude, hid a vast treasure. Many years later, the map showing where the treasure was buried came into the hands of a scruffy pirate chief called Audacious Albert. In a frenzy of excitement, he started to dig for gold!

(chant:) Pi - rates dig for bur - ied trea - sure.

(repeat as necessary)

But however deep he dug, Audacious Albert couldn't find the treasure. In disgust he threw the map away. It was found by another pirate, Dastardly Dick, who dug and dug:

Pi - rates dig for bur - ied trea - sure.

(repeat as necessary)

But Dastardly Dick couldn't find the treasure either. Exhausted, he gave the map to his fiendish friend, Greedy Gordon.

(repeat as necessary)

Pi - rates dig for bur - ied trea - sure.

Greedy Gordon became *very* angry when *he* couldn't find the treasure. He put the map in a bottle and hurled it into the sea.
One day, on a farther shore, a young pirate called Enterprising Egbert saw the map sticking out of the bottle as he walked along a deserted beach. He recognised the island of Vi-O'Lyn straight away, and hurriedly got together a party of four able pirates to set sail for the island and help him dig. Egbert's pirates dug and dug.

(repeat as necessary)

Pi - rates dig for bur - ied trea - sure.

6   Their lazy leader looked on and smirked with glee, because

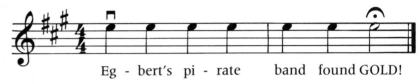

Eg - bert's pi - rate   band   found GOLD!

But the four pirates didn't see why Egbert should have the gold. Even though it was *his* map, *they'd* done all the work!
So they plotted against him. They decided to bury the gold again and keep it for themselves. While unsuspecting Egbert was asleep . . .

Along came the 1st pirate and

bur - ied   his   trea - sure.

(Keep your 1st finger covering the place where the treasure is buried.)

Along came the 2nd pirate and

bur - ied   his   trea - sure.

(Keep your 2nd finger covering the place where the treasure is buried.)

Along came the 3rd pirate and

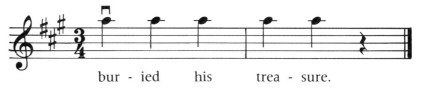

bur - ied his trea - sure.

(Keep your 3rd finger covering the place where the treasure is buried.)

Along came the 4th pirate and, even though he was only very small, he also

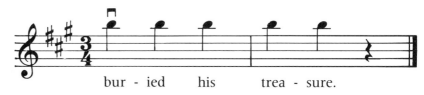

bur - ied his trea - sure.

(Keep your 4th finger covering the place where the treasure is buried. Now all 4 treasure spots should be hidden so that Egbert can't see them.)

When Egbert woke up he was *furious*. He wanted *all* the gold for himself. He brandished his dagger and cried, 'Yo ho ho and a bottle of rum! You wicked, thieving pirates, dig that treasure up again!'

So, the 4th pirate

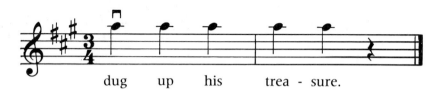

dug up his trea - sure.

(Now you've lifted your 4th finger so you can see the place where the treasure was hidden.)

And the 3rd pirate

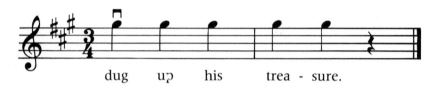

dug up his trea - sure.

(Now you've lifted your 3rd finger so you can see the place where the treasure was hidden.)

Then, the 2nd pirate

dug up his trea - sure.

(Now you've lifted your 2nd finger so you can see the place where the treasure was hidden.)

And even the 1st pirate

dug   up   his   trea - sure.

(Now you've lifted your 1st finger so you can see the place where the treasure was hidden.)

'It's all MY gold now!' gloated Egbert as the other pirates slunk off.
But what none of them ever found were the extra hoards of gold which were also hidden on the map, if you knew where to look . . .

Later, when Egbert was out of the way, the other pirates decided that enough was enough!
'Let's put him in a boat and cast him off to sea,' they whispered. They waited until it was dark (because they weren't very brave) and crept up on Egbert, who was busy counting his gold. They took him prisoner and slung him into a boat. Poor Egbert! – cast off to sea with just a bottle of rum and a half empty tin of ship's biscuits. But the pirates did leave him one small bag of gold, and Polly their parrot for company.

10 Egbert sighed, wishing he hadn't been so greedy. Well, at least this was an adventure!
He lay down in the little boat and looked at the moon and the stars in the sky.
'Do you know this song, Polly?' he asked, and began to sing to keep his spirits up.

Twinkle, twinkle Little Star

Twin - kle, twin - kle   lit - tle   star,   How   I   won - der   what   you   are,

Up   a - bove the   world   so   high,

Like   a   dia - mond   in   the   sky.

Twin - kle, twin - kle,   lit - tle   star,   How   I   won - der   what   you   are.

'I know another song,' squawked Polly, 'all about the light of the moon.'

Au Clair de la Lune

Au clair de la lu - ne, Mon a - mi Pier - rot.
Ouv - re moi ta por - te pour l'a - mour de Dieu.

Prê - te - moi ta plu - me, Pour é - crire un mot.

Ma chand - elle est mor - te, Je n'ai plus de feu.

'Polly!' cried Egbert, applauding, 'what an educated bird you are. I didn't know parrots could speak French!'

At first it was very pleasant at sea, with the wind blowing gently round the boat. But after a while clouds gathered in the sky, and rain began to fall. It was very cold. Egbert shivered and his teeth chattered . . .

(Play ♩ ♩ ♩ ♩ *using the wood of your bow – 'Col Legno'.)*

Then it thundered . . .

I Hear Thunder

I hear thun - der, I hear thun - der. Hark don't you, hark don't you? Pit - ter pat - ter rain drops, pit - ter pat - ter rain drops. I'm wet through! So are you!

As the storm grew fiercer poor Egbert and Polly were tossed higher and higher by the waves.

Storm Exercise

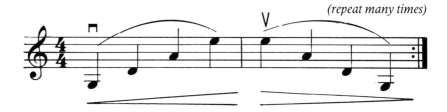

(repeat many times)

(Play the notes slowly and softly at first, then gradually get faster and louder with each repeat. When the storm is past its worst, play gradually slower and softer again, until you end peacefully on an open G.)

But after a few hours, the sea became calm again. To his relief, Egbert spied land ahead. In the far distance he could see buildings clustered round a harbour.
Their roofs were glistening in the sun as they dried out after the rain.
'I must row towards land,' Egbert said, and Polly sang him an encouraging sort of song.

Lightly Row

Light - ly row, light - ly row, to the har - bour we must go.

Light - ly row, light - ly row, we must get there, that we know.

We are sea - sick, tired and wet, ve - ry hun - gry too, but yet,

Light - ly row, light - ly row, to the har - bour we must go.

At last Egbert and Polly managed to land their boat safely. They were tired and bedraggled and very hungry. Where could they find to buy food? Then they heard a cheerful sound. 'Listen!' cried Egbert. 'A Hot Cross Bun Man!'

Hot Cross Buns

Hot cross buns!   Hot cross buns!   One a pen-ny, two a pen-ny, Hot cross buns!

(You can play 'Hot Cross Buns' on the other strings too, using the same pattern of fingering.)

They bought delicious hot cross buns, running with butter, and sat by the roadside to eat them.
'We must make a plan,' said Egbert, licking his fingers when they had finished.

16 'Perhaps we could join a circus,' suggested Polly.
'Don't be SILLY!' snorted Egbert. 'What could *we* do in a circus?
Anyway, the chances of us finding one . . .'
But he never finished his sentence, for around the corner came a
man banging a big bass drum – followed by the saddest elephant you've ever seen.

Bim-Bam Song

Bim - bam, whim wham, beat the drum!

Fine

Here's the cir - cus, full of fun!

Bim - bam, whim wham, beat the drum!

D.C. al Fine

Here's the cir - cus, full of fun!

'Quick, follow them, Polly!' said Egbert. 'Fly on ahead and see where they go. I shall stay here and think.' So while the parrot followed the man from Bim-Bam's Circus, our lazy hero sat down and thought. But thinking was very tiring – especially after all that rowing – so very soon he was fast asleep.

Lullaby

'Squawk, squawk! Wake up, Egbert!'
The pirate opened his eyes and saw Polly flying excitedly round
a man wearing very smart clothes and an elegant top hat. In his
hand he held a poster.
'Ahem! Ahem! I am Mr. Bim-Bam,' he announced in a very
deep voice. 'And this is my circus,' he added, pointing to the
picture.
'I have a problem with my elephant. He is very sad because
some roving vagabonds have stolen his assistant, Percy the
parrot. Now I am looking for another parrot to take his place.
And I need a guard to protect this one. You, Sir,' he said,
pointing to Egbert, 'look a *strong dependable* type.
'What's more, your parrot is just what I am looking for. Will you
and your friend join my troupe? The rate is half a sovereign a
month, with meals. Mrs. Bim-Bam is a *superb* cook.'
'Oh, thank you, sir!' exclaimed Egbert without a moment's
hesitation. 'That sounds an excellent offer! We'll come straight
away.'
So Egbert set about trying to find an act he could join.

Mr. Bim-Bam had a large troupe. Gerald the Lion Tamer looked after three huge lions. Egbert liked the lions, but he thought they were a bit noisy and just a little fierce.
All day long they sang:

The Song of the Lions

Growl, growl, growl, ROAR!   Growl, growl, growl, ROAR!

Growl, growl, growl, growl, growl, growl, growl, growl, growl, ROAR!

He decided to watch instead.
Denise was a very clever juggler, who could throw four balls in the air and keep them spinning. But Egbert knew that even he wasn't clever enough to learn to juggle.

Juggling

Then there was Alice, who walked the tight-rope. Egbert thought this looked *very* hard! Besides, it reminded him of walking the plank.

Walking the Tight-Rope

Oh! There were lots of wonderful acts to choose from . . . but Egbert knew that all the circus people had to practise for hours and hours every day to perfect their skills.

'I can't think of *anything* I would be able to do,' he sighed in despair. But then Mr. Bim-Bam suggested 'Clowning!' Egbert was overjoyed! He watched the clowns rushing about, falling over, getting tricks wrong on purpose, throwing bags of flour at each other, and generally causing all kinds of confusion.

The Clowns

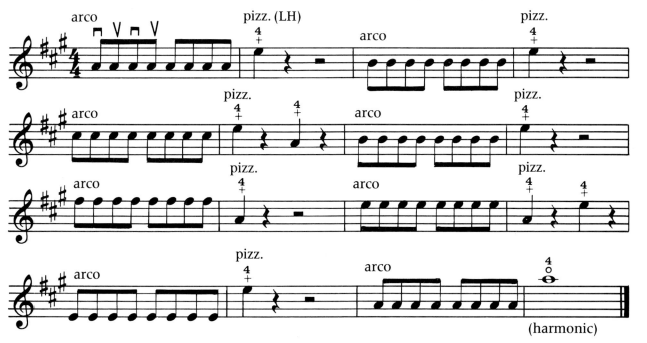

(harmonic)

22 Then Egbert practised with them every day until he was ready to join in a performance. It was very hard work (especially for an ex-rapscallion pirate), but he was enjoying himself so much he didn't mind.

Polly, meanwhile, had learned all the tricks for the elephant act, and was busy cheering up the enormous sad animal.

Sad or Happy March for an Elephant

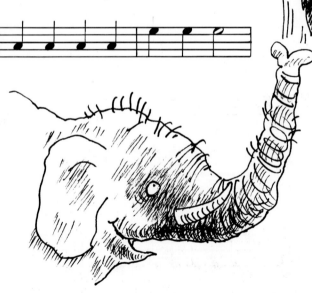

Bim-Bam's Circus travels the countryside,
going from town to town in a grand procession.

Up Hill and Down Dale

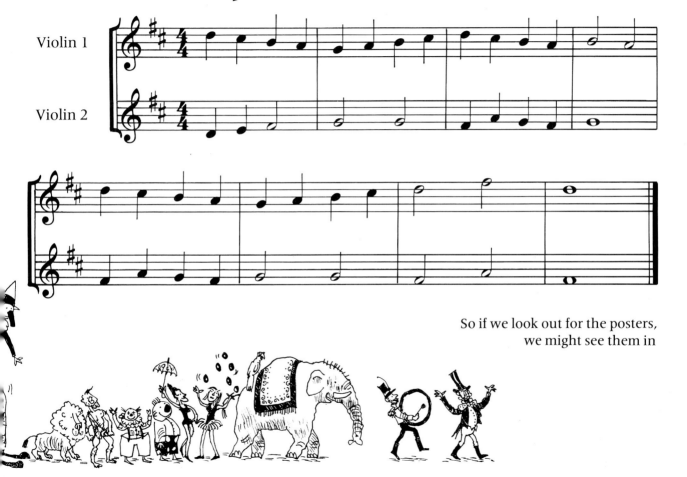

So if we look out for the posters,
we might see them in

our town one day," finished Mother.

"Oh," said Egbert, sadly. "Is that the end? Couldn't we do some more?"

"Tomorrow," said Mother. "But while I'm baking a cake for tea, you could go and dress up as a pirate or clown. Or you could make a parrot, or some treasure, or paint a poster for the circus or . . ."

But Egbert wasn't listening! He'd already dashed upstairs to see what he could find.